E S C APE

from the

COCOON

The true story of how a
near-death experience
in the wilderness of
Alaska propelled
the transformation
of one man who
despised religion
into a warrior
for Christ.

J. Martin Eichhorn

Outskirts Press, Inc.
Denver, Colorado

Outskirts Press, Inc.
http://www.outskirtspress.com

ISBN: 978-1-4327-3072-7

Library of Congress Control Number: 2008940601

Outskirts Press and the "OP" logo are trademarks belonging to Outskirts Press, Inc.

PRINTED IN THE UNITED STATES OF AMERICA

Contents

Acknowledgments

I owe my life to Jesus Christ. May I learn well how to lose my life for His sake. Thank you, Jesus, for all you have done. Amen.

And thank you, honey, for your unwavering support of all that I do. It has been more than exciting to become one with you. May our love continue to grow with each day, bringing us all the fullness of knowing God through His love for us and our deep abiding love for each other. Muwah, honey!

To my dearest daughters, Addie and Rosie; here it is, girls! Your Pappa's story! You have far more to do with my story than you realize. Words cannot describe the depth of inspiration you bring to my life. I'm so proud of you both, just the way you are. I love you sooooooooooo MUCH!

A deep, heartfelt gratitude goes out to the wonderful orphaned children of *Atlantis* and the adults who take care of them. I will never forget you. Your yearning for the Lord inspires my faith beyond measure. Your love of Jesus is contagious!

Finally, a great thank you to my Christian brother, artist Robert Kevin Meyers. This book would not be in print without your encouragement, bro. May your wishes be met in that this book touches the lives of many.

Prologue

This book is a true story of the spiritual journey of my life. It is the story of events in my life that facilitated my transformation from a person who turned his back on God and despised religion, into a follower of Jesus Christ. My story includes a near-death experience in the wilds of Alaska that gave me faith in the existence of God and life after death. Yet that is just the beginning. It wasn't until 23 years after the near-death experience that I really began to seek God with all my heart. Even though I've had many other instances where my life was on the line, including being interrogated with a knife at my throat by a band of communist rebels in the Philippines, it took being totally and completely broken before a real change in me occurred. And that is the rest of the story.

I hope and pray that my story will serve to inspire others to strengthen their relationship with God and Jesus Christ. May my story encourage those who are already sold out for Christ, and may those who are still not sure about the existence of God and Jesus be given hope and inspiration to continue seeking Him.

Near-death experiences are a phenomenon that perplexes the human mind. A glimpse of that which lies beyond this life intrigues the imagination. For some it gives hope for life after death; others remain skeptical of the meaning behind such experiences. As for myself, I, too, was doubtful of the reality behind what others have described when they were on the verge of death or actually pronounced dead by physicians. That is until I experienced the onset of death in 1980.

Almost all near-death experiences that I am aware of have involved spirituality and/or religious beliefs to some extent. In order to fully appreciate my own near-death experience, I believe it is important to first examine the state of my spiritual being leading up to the experience. The events going on in my life just prior to my near-death experience were somewhat spectacular. Therefore, I believe it is important to provide a general review of my spirituality along with a more detailed explanation of the events leading up to my bout with death in order to gain an understanding of my state of mind at the time. I hope that this understanding will help to add clarity to the reality of what I witnessed as I was dying.

But there is so much more to the story. Obtaining a strong faith in God and in the existence of heaven is just the beginning. That is where the journey begins…

In The Beginning

As a young boy growing up in the Midwest, my parents would occasionally take me to church. We attended several Episcopal churches, and I disliked every one of them. In fact, I hated going to church. Just the thought of having to wear nice clothes and go to where I had to sit still and be quiet for an hour and a half turned me off. I believed that the weekends were made for young boys to go out and play and explore the outdoors. Church was not my idea of a good way to spend a Sunday morning.

At least, while resisting the boredom of church service, I heard stories about a man named Jesus – the Son of God. I was told that if I believed in Him, I would be saved and have everlasting life. That sounded pretty good to me. As a young boy primarily interested in sports and nature, the thought of not having to worry about death was appealing to me. So I decided to believe in the things that I was told about this man named Jesus. It all made perfect sense to me, and I liked the idea that when someone died they went to a nice place called heaven.

And so life went on for me with no major trials or distractions from my pursuits of playing sports and enjoying the wonders of nature. In fact, the more I observed nature the more it made sense to me that there really was a God who created all things.

This idea drove home in my mind one day as I watched a group of ants working around their hill. Some ants were dragging pebbles down into their home. They would bump into other ants who were hauling pebbles out of their home. Perhaps, I thought, the ants carrying pebbles out of their home were the females who were picking up after the males that were carrying pebbles into their homes. A few ants worked together to drag a dead grasshopper, many times larger than they, across the ground and stuff it into the hole of their home. There were so many ants, all of them very busy and intent on what they were doing. Most of the time I could not figure out what it was they were doing, but all of them seemed to have a job, and they would go nonstop until the job was done. I would stare at and observe the ants for hours, wondering, *How do they know what to do?* Then it hit me, God created them and somehow programmed them to do the things they do. That made perfect sense.

I began to marvel at many other aspects of life. Every spring I would go to a pond a few miles from my house and collect gallons of pond water containing lots of tadpoles. Keeping them throughout the summer, I would replenish their pond water often. The miracle of life appeared right before my eyes as I watched them gradually transform into frogs. By the end of the summer I had a whole herd of frogs to take back to the pond to release! Now, how could those tadpoles know how to do that if they weren't created by God to do so?

The wonders of metamorphosis captured my curiosity, especially through watching caterpillars turn into butterflies. Along with my tadpole collection I also had several caterpillars that I fed and cared for during the summer. I'd sit for hours and watch them spin their cocoons in the fall. Round and round they went, weaving long strands of thread around themselves until they were completely encompassed and closed in. Through the winter I would stare at the cocoons and wonder what was going on inside. Then on one glorious day the following spring, the much-anticipated event occurred as I witnessed the incredible emergence of Monarch butterflies and Cecropia moths from the cocoons! This marvel of nature had to be proof of the existence of God!

Doubt Settles In

But then something happened shortly after my 13th birthday that shattered my unwavering belief in God. The year was 1970. The Vietnam war had been waging for most of my young life. I saw pictures of the horrors of that war on television and in magazines. Body bags holding dead soldiers that were gently unloaded from airplanes—it was a sight I could not get out of my mind. Some relatives of my buddies who were strapping young men never returned home from that war. Still I hung on to my belief that there was this awesome God who was taking care of the fallen soldiers in heaven. But then everything changed one night when my parents and I went to my dad's boss's house for dinner.

The Tices were very nice people. It was obvious that Dad had a good relationship with his boss, Mr. Tice. When we entered their home that night for dinner, I noticed a picture of a very handsome young man in uniform proudly displayed in a place of honor in the living room. Surrounding the photograph were several medals. I was strangely drawn to that young man in the photograph. After brief introductions, everyone left the room except for Mrs. Tice and me; perhaps she noticed that I couldn't take my eyes off that picture.

I asked her, "Who is the man in this picture?"

"Oh," Mrs. Tice replied, "that's our son."

"Where is he now?" I replied, eager to see if I could meet him.

Just then Mrs. Tice's eyes became hollow, and with a horrifying look that I had never seen before she replied, "He was killed in Vietnam." Then she hurried out of the room.

Alone in the room, I couldn't keep from staring at the photograph of Mrs. Tice's son. As I stood there looking into his eyes in the picture I tried to imagine what he was like. He really wasn't that much older than I was. He looked like he could have been one of my buddies. I tried to imagine what had happened to him, just how he died. Visions of the horrible scenes of the war that I had seen on television and in magazines began to enter into my mind. Then I peered over the medals beside his picture. A Purple Heart was there. Looking back into the eyes in the picture I saw the same horrifying look in his mom's eyes that I had seen moments before. I became overwhelmed with sadness. My cheeks grew wet from tears. Then I felt an enormous rush of anger welling up inside me. I became angry at God.

In my mind I started yelling at God. *How could you allow this to happen? How could you allow this handsome young man to die? Don't you know you sapped the joy out of his mother's life? Why do you let wars happen, anyway? Either you don't have all this power some people say you have, or you don't really love us at all!*

The doubting began. Nothing made sense anymore.

If God truly has the power to create the world and give caterpillars the ability to turn into butterflies then surely he has the power to stop wars. And if He has all this power and doesn't use it to stop wars then He truly doesn't love us. So, I reasoned, either God is not the all-powerful and loving being that I've been taught about all my life, or He doesn't really exist. Either way, God no longer seemed worthy of my praise and time. Perhaps, I thought, it's time to re-evaluate life, realizing that there is no God, a creator of heaven and earth who truly loves us.

And so I turned my back on God. What did it matter since He probably didn't really exist, anyway? The next few years of my life were rather empty. I focused my energy on sports. I argued with my parents about going to church. I began to fear death. But still, something deep down inside me wanted to believe in God. Sometimes I'd lie awake at night and ask Him to show me a sign that He really was out there, somewhere. *Please, God, please,* I'd plead in my mind, *just show me a sign that you're really there. Anything that is obvious it comes from you. Please, God, please...* I received no answer from God — at least not then…

In Search
Of The Truth

My high school years went on, filled with all the excitement and pleasures that one can get from this world. Successes in high school sports gave me a great deal of confidence in myself. I achieved a lot — all without the help of God. I became quite full of myself. Yet my spirit was empty.

In order to find the answer to my question regarding the existence of God, I decided to read the Bible, beginning with page one. I never made it to the end of Genesis. My old version of King James was too confusing; I kept getting bogged down in trying to read the sentences over and over, trying to understand what was being said. That form of English was just too hard for me to understand. If the Bible really was the inspired word of God, then why did He make it so hard to understand? Out of my own ignorance, I had no idea that there were other, more comprehensible versions of the Bible. Henceforth, I gave up on searching for answers in Scripture.

Observing people in church and organized religion in general really turned me off of what Christianity appeared to be. In many self-proclaimed Christians I saw the arrogance of a "holier than thou" attitude. And oh so many hypocrites! What is the deal with all those exuberant churches and cathedrals, anyway? I thought Jesus was supposed to be an advocate for the poor. Wouldn't He have wanted the money they used to build extravagant buildings to be spent on meeting the needs of people?

I resented the way most churches seemed to feed off of people's guilt to extort money from them by passing a plate or basket in front of them during the Sunday service. It made going to church seem like going to a movie; pay your money and see the show. Why would people pay good money for an hour or two of boredom, anyway?

And another thing, many of the most vicious wars in human history were fought over differences in religious beliefs. Obviously it seemed the world would be a much better place if the whole idea of religion were somehow erased from human consciousness. Therefore, I reasoned, perhaps I would be better off to eliminate religion from my life.

In an attempt to feed my spirit I began to study philosophy. I voraciously read many authors such as Plato and his dialogue with Socrates, Aristotle, Descartes, Kant, Hume, Mills, Locke, and many others. Existentialism fascinated me. Yet still I had a yearning to discover the truth about the existence of God. Though I had turned my back on Him, there was still something deep inside me that wanted to believe. If He would just show me a sign…

With my mind filled with philosophical explanation and a

study of logic, I produced a line of reasoning in my approach to answer the question about the truth of the existence of God. It went something like this:

If I believe in God and He does exist, then when I die everything will be wonderful.

If I believe in God and He does not exist, then when I die nothing happens.

If I don't believe in God and He does not exist, then when I die nothing happens.

If I don't believe in God and He does exist, then when I die I'm in big trouble!

Therefore, I concluded, it would be logical for me to start believing in God again, just in case He really does exist. So I started to sort of half believe in God, but I did not change anything about my daily life's pursuit of pleasures of this world, nor did I read the Bible or enter into fellowship with those who truly believed. It's like I wanted to believe in God for my own salvation at death just in case He was real, but I didn't want to have anything to do with churchgoers nor with what believers are supposed to do. My heart still remained troubled and empty, longing for a sign from God…

And then it came, in the year 1980. I was 23 years old. I was a junior in college and some of my old high school buddies were driving up to Alaska to work for the US Geological Survey. They asked if I wanted to go along and maybe I could find work up there for the summer. My answer was a resounding YES!

The Quest
Of A Lifetime

W e left the day after I took my last final exam. It took 12 days to drive to Anchorage from Madison, Wisconsin. We stayed a couple extra nights in campgrounds near Banff, British Columbia, Laird Hot Springs near the border of British Columbia and the Yukon, and Dawson City, Yukon. It was the trip of a lifetime filled with adventure and oh so many stories to tell!

The day came when I had to depart from my traveling companions. They had to begin work, and I had to begin looking for work. My plan was to look for work on commercial fishing boats, or possibly hire on with a drilling rig, and if all else failed surely I could get a job in a cannery. My friends dropped me off at the end of the AlCan Highway; the Homer Spit. Equipped with a small tent, a few camping supplies, a little food, and maybe $200, I set up camp on the beach, bid my friends farewell, and began dreaming of the days to come.

Early the next morning I arose from my tent and immediately walked down to the docks, going from boat to boat, asking for a job. The answer I received from every ship's captain was the same. The fishermen were all on strike — even the shrimp boats were not running — and so all the canneries were closed. Apparently the Japanese had flooded the US market with tons of fish, so the price the fishermen were offered for their catch was not worth the effort. Hopefully, though, things would be resolved in a week or so and then there would be plenty of work available.

After about a week of no change in the strike I became very antsy. My food and money started to dwindle to the point where I needed to do something. Camping on the Homer Spit became less than exciting. I had heard that the fishermen on Kodiak Island would likely be the first to go back to fishing, and maybe even a few shrimp boats had started making their runs. It seemed logical to me that Kodiak Island was where I needed to be. So I boarded the ferry and settled in for the 20-hour ride to Kodiak.

At about 4 a.m., I walked off the ferry into the town of Kodiak. The sun was up but all the businesses were closed. The air was damp and cold. The streets of the small town were totally empty. I had never felt so alone in all my life. And I was very hungry. I was beginning to wonder if I had made the right decision.

After a two-hour wait in the cold, damp air I hustled into a restaurant as soon as the doors opened for business. I needed to warm up and fill my belly with a good breakfast. Now I was ready for the docks to continue my pursuit of work.

But the story with the fishermen here was the same as that at Homer — the strike was still on with no end in sight.

Not even the shrimp boats were running and the canneries were closed. My situation was bordering on the line of desperation. Scared, yes, I was very scared, and oh so lonely, yet I felt a strong sense of adventure, and I knew it was time I proved to myself that I really was as strong and tough as I thought I was. I was going to see if I could survive the wilds of Alaska depending only on myself, as I had left God behind years ago.

The first thing to do was find a map of the area, which the Forest Service provided me. There was a river a few miles out of town, perhaps a good place to set up camp and wait out the strike. Sure enough it was. In fact, the river was full of fish as the red salmon were running! And the bushes along the banks of the river were covered with salmon berries! Like a bear getting ready for a long winter's sleep I bloated myself with salmon and berries. Mmm, what a life!

After a few days of pure gluttony, reality began to sink in and I decided it was time to go back into town to check on the situation with the strike. Once in town I discovered that the strike was still on with no end in sight. For some reason that I can't explain, I felt a strong desire to go to the Kodiak airport. It was a typical scene one finds at any airport, many people of various ages scurrying around about their business. But then I noticed a group of three young men who stood out from the crowd. They looked a little bewildered, and it was obvious that they were, like me, some college kids who had come to Alaska to find work for the summer. Sure enough I was right.

After a brief introduction I informed them of the strike and invited them out to my camp where they could fill their bellies with fresh salmon and berries. Once they confirmed my story about the strike, I had new companions for the journey of my life: Chuck, Corey, and Tony, all from Oregon.

There seemed to be no end to the salmon run. For days we feasted to our hearts' content. Every few days or so, a couple of us would go into Kodiak to check on the strike. The news was always the same — no end in sight.

Eventually the salmon stopped running. We were now in a very precarious predicament. Short on food, with little or no money and not much hope for work to become available soon, we decided it was time for a move.

We studied our maps of the island and decided it was time to trek to a place on the map called Ugak Bay. About 15 miles from the town of Kodiak was a trail that would take us there. We figured that maybe we could find food there for another week or two and maybe, just maybe, after that amount of time, maybe the strike would be over and we could finally get some jobs. So, we four college kids from the lower 48 packed up camp and hitch-hiked our way to the trailhead that would lead us on the 13-mile trek to Ugak Bay.

It was unimaginably beautiful. We counted over 30 pairs of bald eagles that were nesting in the trees around our camp at the edge of the ocean. Mountain peaks filled the horizon to the north, the bright blue ocean to the south. In the hills behind our camp we found rabbits, beaver, deer, and bear tracks that were so huge that Corey's Ruger 48 caliber pistol with an eight-inch barrel fit completely within the pad print. The nail prints of that bear track were at least six inches long. We were camping in the territory of the infamous giant Kodiak bear!

Lost

It was glorious! Day after day we took our fill from the land. The mountains in our backyard provided a playground beyond belief. I never tired of watching the bald eagles go about their daily routine. Life was very good.

But as they say, eventually all good things must come to an end. After about a week or so (I lost track of the days) our supply of food began to run low. The streams near camp no longer provided the daily catch of fish, and we had depleted the local supply of rabbits. Yet we were not ready to leave this awesome place. We decided to split up and go on a massive search for food.

Corey decided to go back into the mountain valleys north of camp to search for game. Chuck was nursing a sprained ankle, so he was going to fish around camp. Tony and I headed north along the seashore hoping to find a river that, according to our map, was three coves over and would lead us to Lake Miam. We thought we could trek to the lake and test the fishing opportunities there and return back to camp in one day. Our collective success in our search for food would determine how much longer we could stay in this unbelievably pristine place.

The tide was out, exposing a huge expanse of seashore, as Tony and I ventured along the beach. Alaska has some of the largest tide changes in the world. It seemed to us that the ocean was at least half a mile away from us when previously it would have been right at our feet.

After several hours of hiking we still had not reached the mouth of the river that we thought would take us to Lake Miam. Tony began to realize that the lake was much farther away from us than what it appeared to be on our map. He was ready to return back to camp. But not me. I was bound and determined to find that lake in hopes that it would be brimming with fish so that we could remain in this wonderland. And so, after bidding farewell to Tony, I pressed onward.

An hour or so later I began to get frustrated. I still had not come upon the mouth of the river. The thought occurred to me that if I could climb up the cliffs of the shoreline and make it to the top I could cut cross country heading northeast and eventually reach the river. After taking a few minutes to study the cliffs, I saw a place that looked like it could be climbable. I judged the distance in height to be about 60 feet straight up. I decided to go for it.

I found myself in a real jam about ten feet from the top. The vertical from that point on was too steep. Going back down was not an option. One false move would plunge me 50 feet down to the rocky bottom. If I were to fall and break a leg or ankle, I would be stuck there for who knows how long. My only option was to continue on somehow. By digging my fingernails into soil between the cliff rocks I was able to inch my way up. About five feet from the top there were some roots of bushes poking through cracks in the rocks. At one point I had to grab hold of a root by my teeth while my feet were frantically trying to find something to rest on. Blood drained from my fingertips as they desperately dug into soil and rock. Inch by grueling inch I edged my way closer. Eventually, somehow, I made it to the top. *Whew!*

Once on top I took a moment to look down the path I had just climbed. I realized how crazy I was to even attempt such a climb! Then I looked out over the ocean and took a deep breath of the salty air. By now, I guessed, I had been away from camp for about six hours. Still anxious to find that river and the treasure of fish that I was certain it would lead me to, I was ready to continue on. I studied the mountains for bearings and looked for a route that I believed would take me toward the river. It couldn't be too far away, I reasoned. Away I went.

Soon the terrain turned from grassy hillsides to a thick covering of monster-size sagebrush-like bushes. These bushes were much taller than I was, and I had to meander my way through them. They went on and on and on and on. Then I realized…it was perfect cover for the infamous Kodiak bears that I knew were in the area! A brief flash of doom pierced through my body at the thought of surprising one. It took awhile for me to regain my composure. Then my drive to find fish returned. Fighting my fear of spooking up a monster Kodiak bear I pressed on.

All of a sudden a storm blew in from the ocean. It was upon me before I could see it coming. Almost immediately I was surrounded by a dense fog with a light misty rain. I could feel the temperature drop. The mountains were hidden by the fog, and I lost my bearings. I pushed myself forward with only a pretense of where I was going.

With both the fog and giant sagebrush getting thicker, I became disoriented. Walking with any sense of direction was impossible. Why I didn't see it, I don't know. But I fell into a big hole in the ground. After brushing the wet dirt off me I saw them…huge, fresh prints of the feet of a Kodiak bear in the dirt! My flight response kicked in, and I was out of that hole instantly! Was the bear nearby? I had no way of knowing for sure. Perhaps for the first time in several hours I came to my senses. It was time for me to surrender my quest for food and head back to camp. The problem was — in which direction was camp?

It seemed logical to assume that if I started walking at a right angle to my left that I would be headed in the general direction of camp. So off in that direction I went. After what seemed to be one or two hours of pushing through wet monster bushes I came to another big hole in the ground. I peered down into the hole to see if I could see bear tracks. What I found sent a chill throughout my body. Next to giant bear tracks at the bottom of the hole were my own footprints. I had been walking in a huge circle for hours!

Wet, cold, and oh so hungry, I was completely lost. I came to the realization that I had no idea in which direction were the mountains or the ocean. The fog was a thick soup of misty rain, and I could not see past the bushes right in front of me. I sat for a moment to ponder my situation. All of me felt damp and cold and lonely. It was obvious that I had to keep moving in order to keep my body temperature up. If I could only find my way back to the ocean I could walk on top of the ridge of the cliffs back to camp. Maybe I could find a way down to the shoreline and have easier walking. I decided my best chance of finding the ocean was to keep walking downhill.

Eventually I stumbled upon a tiny creek, which I followed. Sure enough, it led me to the edge of the cliffs where it trickled down to the shoreline. By that time it was starting to get dark, which told me that it was well past midnight. I'd had enough of walking through the dense, wet bushes and fog. My mind was focused on getting back to camp, sitting by the fire with something warm to eat and drink. If I stayed on top I might end up wandering directionless all night. If I could climb down this little waterfall to the ocean I could be back to camp in a few hours.

The first half of the climb down the little waterfall was fairly easy, although slick in spots. But then the little rocks that supported me gave way, and I slid down the rest of the way. Neither the toes of my boots nor the tips of my fingers could dig in enough to break my fall. Luckily I landed on the shoreline with only scrapes and bruises but no broken bones. I made it!

To my astonishment, the ocean was only about three feet from the edge of the cliffs. The tide had come in while I was wandering around aimlessly up on top. Waves pounded the beach with anger at my feet. At least I was on flat ground with no more monster bushes in my path. My spirit lifted as I headed back to camp.

In The Face
Of Death

Walking along the sheer cliffs with the ocean only a
few feet away, I came to a huge rock outcropping
that was jutting way out into the ocean. I had no idea how
deep the water was surrounding the outcrop. My first
thought was to try and climb over it. After several attempts
I realized that was not possible as the rock face was too flat
and steep. By this time I was anxious, extremely tired, cold,
and hungry, and just sitting there waiting for the tide to go
back out was not an option. Somehow I had to get back to
camp. The thought occurred to me that maybe I could jump
in the ocean and swim around the rock outcropping and back
to the narrow shoreline on the other side. Wearing a denim
jacket and hiking boots, with my camera strapped around
my neck and fishing pole in one hand, I jumped into the
ocean.

Almost immediately I felt an enormous pull, like
something had grabbed a hold of my feet, which pulled me

down and out. It was as though lead weights were strapped to my feet. I was caught in the undertow of the tide. I began to struggle, kicking my feet and paddling frantically with my arms, trying to fight the pull of the tide. But it didn't work. I kept moving farther down and out.

Fighting the pull of the tide, I couldn't hold my breath any longer. Unable to resist the urge to breathe, I inhaled. The sting of icy-cold salty water hit my lungs. Another urge to take a breath overcame me, and this time as I inhaled I felt an icy-cold stinging chill rush all throughout my body.

Instantly a new sensation filled my body. The stinging chill turned to a feeling of warmth and contentment. The feeling was so strong and good that I began to think that drowning was not so bad after all. In fact, I rather liked it. It must be what people mean when they talk about euphoria. *Maybe I should just let go and let the ocean take me,* I thought.

Just then, in the darkness of my mind, I saw a point of light way off in the distance. The light grabbed my attention as it grew larger and brighter. It quickly developed into a tunnel of light, similar to that of a flashlight, with a beam of light emanating from a glowing, radiating source of light. I couldn't take my attention off the light as it was all that was in my mind besides the darkness. The beam transformed itself into a cone-shaped tunnel of light, with the tip of the cone pinpointed at the light's origin. The sides of the cone-shaped tunnel of light were like tiny particles that danced and glowed and flickered like stars, with brilliance like nothing I had ever seen before. Physical descriptions using adjectives and metaphors simply cannot adequately explain the experience. It was more like I could *sense* and *feel* the tunnel of light rather than see it. Somehow I knew it was there and knew what it looked like without actually seeing it with open eyes, with a perception going beyond imagination or memory.

It was all very strange, surreal. Here I was drowning, but I felt warm and fuzzy and content beyond belief, as if I were filled to the brim of all wants and desires. I felt a complete satisfaction, with a joy that defies description. Then this strange tunnel of light appeared in my mind and captured my full attention; I was totally oblivious to what was happening to me physically. I had a strong sense that this tunnel of light was the way home, somehow the route to heaven, and all I needed to do was let go of this life and let it take me…

Something at the end of the tunnel started to move toward me. It got larger as it came closer to me. Soon it was right in front me — the face of my mother's mother, Granny. The image of her face was as clear as if she were actually right there before me. I could see every line on her face and the intensity in her deep blue eyes. She just stood there staring at me. Here I was drowning, filled with warmth and peace, staring into the face of my mother's mother, which appeared in a tunnel of light emanating from what I believed to be heaven. I was confused. What did Granny have to do with all this?

In a flash Granny's face vanished. I know it sounds strange, but I began to hear a whisper of a voice in my mind calling me to follow Jesus. Like all I needed to do was follow the voice through the tunnel of light and I would find Jesus. The voice was unlike any voice I had heard before, very soft and angelic, with a kind of musical tone yet not really musical; it had a calming effect on me. Yet I didn't really *hear* the voice, it was more that I just knew it was there and felt its presence, kind of like the light in that I didn't really see it but knew that it was there. It seemed as though the door of heaven lay open before me; the voice and the light were the path to follow. Clearly, in my mind at that time, I was given a choice. I could focus on the warm, contented feeling and let myself enter into death and follow the voice that led to Jesus, or I could reject the voice and end up who knows where. The strange thing is that I had the distinct notion that even though I would be drowned and my body long gone, there would still be me to continue on.

Then I began to see faint images of my parents, family, and friends. These images were not so clear, kind of blurry, but I could make out who the people were. A desire to see them again welled up inside me as I realized I was drowning. Heaven seemed great and warm and beautiful, full of contentment, but I wasn't ready for that yet. I wanted to live.

My situation was desperate. I was within grasp of heaven. If Jesus was really there perhaps He would help me, I thought. It wasn't as if I believed that Jesus was really there; it was more like *He had to be* as my only hope for life. In my mind I began crying out to Jesus with all of my strength and energy. *Help me, Jesus, help me!* I cried over and over again in my mind. *Help me, Jesus, help me!* I concentrated on those words until there was nothing left in my mind except *Help me, Jesus! I am drowning in the ocean near Ugak Bay, Kodiak Island, southern Alaska, in the northwest corner of North America, planet earth, help me, Jesus, hellllllllllllllp ppppppppp me!*

Instantly my head was above the water and I was coughing

my brains out. I have no idea how it happened — it just did. I couldn't believe it, I was still alive! With each breath of air I coughed uncontrollably. Every time I gasped for air I'd start coughing so hard I couldn't breathe. But how did I get here? My head was above water in an instant, but I felt no pull or push against my body. Could Jesus really have lifted me up? When I realized how far away from shore I was, my mind had to focus on the matter at hand. After a while (I have no idea how long) of coughing and gasping for each breath of air, I finally was able to breathe without coughing. I began to swim back to shore. Somehow I had the strength within me to make it.

Once on shore I turned around and looked back over the ocean, thinking about what just happened and the images I saw in my mind. As I tried to understand the meaning of the images and discern if I had actually been saved by Jesus, I realized I was shivering uncontrollably. Amazingly my camera was still around my neck, and my hand was holding my fishing pole. But I had a new problem. Soaking wet to the bone, I was in serious danger of hyperthermia. I removed my clothing and wrung it out with my hands as best as I could. After putting my cold, damp clothes back on I started doing exercises to try and increase my body heat. Pangs of an empty stomach sapped my ability to keep it up for long. I was completely exhausted.

I decided to walk along the narrow beach away from the rock outcropping and came to a huge crack in the cliffs that formed a small cave. Huddling inside the cave I mustered up every ounce of energy I had left to fight the desire to fall asleep. I knew if I let myself fall asleep that I may not wake up due to hyperthermia. As I curled up in a ball shivering, I began to wonder if Jesus could save me again.

After what seemed to be an eternity, the misty rain ceased and the sky began to clear. I desperately wanted to get back to camp. The ocean was still hugging the rock outcropping, and there was no way I was going to jump into the ocean and try to swim around it again. My only hope seemed to be to hike back to that little waterfall where I slid down to the ocean, and try to climb back up through it to the top of the cliffs. It was a gnarly, death-defying climb but I made it. Once on top, the fog had lifted and I could see the mountains.

With the mountains as my guide I began to trudge my way through the giant bushes back to camp. I didn't even think about the possibility of spooking up any bears. All I could think about was taking one step at a time toward camp. After several hours of plodding along, I made it.

It was late in the morning the day after I left camp that I finally stumbled back in. My companions in camp were so glad to see me! Two of them were just about to leave on the all-day journey back to the town of Kodiak to report me as missing to the authorities. Immediately they stoked the fire and put something on for me to eat. After I changed clothes and curled up in my sleeping bag, Tony and Corey came into my tent and lay next to me until I stopped shivering. Minutes later Chuck woke me up with a cup of warm stew and coffee. I slept till the next day.

Obviously it was time for us to leave this incredible place. We were almost out of food and again anxious to find work. After a day of rest for me, we packed up camp and went back to the town of Kodiak. I never told my companions about the near-death experience as I was afraid that they might think I was crazy.

The Letter From Mom

S adly, upon returning to Kodiak, we learned that the fishermen's strike was still on, and not even the canneries were hiring. It was now the first week in July. I decided to call a lead about a potential job working on a core drilling rig that I received while we camped outside of Dawson City, Yukon, on our way to Alaska.

This lead came from a guy who I saw fall out of a tree just outside of Dawson. I ran over to him to see if he was all right. It turned out that his father was a geologist who knew of a drilling company that might be hiring. I had called the company before my friends dropped me off on the Homer Spit about a month earlier, and at that time the driller told me to call him back the first part of July if I still wanted a job. So I called him from Kodiak, and he hired me over the phone to work on his rig north of Nome, near the Arctic Circle. I had to get myself to Anchorage immediately, and he would meet me there.

In Anchorage I spent a night at Gary's house. Gary was a good friend of one of my friends who I came to Alaska with. We used Gary's house as a base in Anchorage, and it is also where I received mail. Waiting for me at Gary's house was a letter from my mom.

Tears welled up in my eyes as I read Mom's letter. She told of how her mother, Granny, had passed away a few days before she wrote the letter. This news hit me like a ton of bricks. Granny's was the face I saw in the tunnel of light while I was drowning. She was dead at the time and I didn't know it. I pondered that thought. As I read Mom's letter over and over, it dawned on me that this had to be the sign from God that I had been praying for in my younger years. There simply was no other explanation as to why I would see the face of Granny when I was near death.

This explanation is more plausible when one understands my relationship with Granny. For all my life that I knew her, Granny was simply a bitter old woman. We (my family) all loved her for who she was, but we didn't really like her. She always seemed to be in a bad mood and was quick to agitate those around her. Often she would make hurtful remarks to people, seemingly not caring about their feelings. She made it clear to everyone as to who in the family was her favorite, and everyone else was made to feel inferior. I was one of the many inferior ones in her eyes. Of all four of my grandparents, whom I knew and loved very much, Granny was the one I liked the least.

It is highly unlikely that in my last moments of life here on earth I would think about Granny, especially to the point where I could see the image of her face in real-life clarity in my mind's eye as I was drowning. The only reasonable conclusion of what I experienced while drowning was that there really is life of some sort after death, and that somehow in death Granny was able to reach me from that which lies beyond this life. It was as if God had sent Granny down from heaven to check on my situation.

Perhaps it is just a coincidence that I would see the face of my dead grandmother as I was dying, even though I didn't know she was dead at the time. I was, at that time unknowingly, looking into the face of death. Perhaps it is also just a coincidence that in the moment I cried out to Jesus to save me from drowning, my head appeared above the water. But at some point one has to realize that too many extraordinary coincidences are beyond mere coincidence.

The following is a list of some of the coincidences leading up to my near-death experience. Some may seem rather small in scope, and others are rather extraordinary. The point being that all these things had to occur in order for me to get to the time and place for the experience to occur:

1. 1980 just happened to be the year commercial fishermen in Alaska were on an extended strike during the time that I was there, which was the reason I went to Kodiak Island.
2. For some reason I felt drawn to visit the airport in Kodiak on a day I just happened to be in town to check on the status of the strike. It is then that I met the guys with whom I went to Ugak Bay; I would not have ventured to Ugak Bay by myself.
3. It just so happened that the tide was out on the morning we went on a massive search for food; the tide was not out like that every day. The timing was perfect for the

tide to be fully in during the time I was desperately trying to get back to camp, which led me to jump into the ocean to try and swim around the outcropping of rock.

4. A storm blew in from the ocean shortly after I climbed to the top of the cliffs. The dense fog prevented me from seeing the mountains; I lost my bearings, which made me go back to the ocean shoreline.

5. I saw a crystal-clear image of my grandmother's face when I was drowning, and I didn't know at the time that she was dead.

6. As soon as I cried out for Jesus to help me, my head was above water.

7. I just happened to be in the right place (Dawson City, Yukon, of all places) at the right time (2:30 a.m.) to see a man fall out of a tree, which is how I eventually found a job. Coincidently, the company that hired me did not need my help until after the time of my near-death experience.

My spiritual status when the near-death experience occurred was somewhat empty. At that point in time I was not a believer. I hadn't been to church in many years, none of my friends were believers, and I was ignorant of Scripture. I feared death, was doubtful of the existence of God, and despised organized religion. In more ways than one I was lost, exhausted, and desperate with only one thought on my mind, which was to make it back to camp.

Both from a logical point of view and from a deep inner gut feeling, I believe that what I experienced while drowning was a sign from Almighty God that He really does exist and that there really is life after death. And, that Jesus Christ is the Savior of my life. God had to prepare me for the experience in order for me to be in a time and place where He could reach me through my deceased grandmother. I had to be totally exhausted, both physically and emotionally, in order for me to cry out to Him with all my heart.

I believe that God planned all of the events leading up to my near-death experience. This message rings loud and clear and true and is a far more reasonable explanation of what happened to me than considering the string of events as mere coincidence. There were simply too many coincidences that occurred at the right time and in the right place for me to believe that all aspects of the near-death experience were just mere coincidence.

But this is only just the beginning. Obtaining proof of life after death and a profound faith in the existence of God were not enough to change me. The remarkable things that God has done in my life since the drowning incident make up the rest of the amazing story.

The Invincible Me

After leaving Kodiak Island, with the brief stop in Anchorage where I read Mom's letter, I ended up in a base camp near Kougarok Mountain — about 100 miles north of Nome, out in the middle of Nowhere. The camp was there to support a core drilling operation that my company was engaged in on the mountain. We were on the verge of discovering the largest deposit of tin in North America.

Fortunately for me when I first arrived in camp, we had a few days of downtime as we were waiting for parts to arrive for the drilling rig before we could begin work. This gave me the opportunity to reflect on what had happened on Kodiak. I climbed to the top of a small mountain near camp where I paid tribute to the life of Granny and prayed to God. It became clear to me that I had been given a great gift in this life: the gift of proof in the existence of God and of life after death. Perhaps more importantly, I began to realize that there was so much more to life than what we perceive with our senses. The reality of a non-physical existence, which

I read about in my philosophy classes in school, began to make sense to me.

I began to develop a close relationship with God, talking to Him often. But, I did not seek to learn more about God through the Bible, nor did I attend a church or fellowship with other believers. It was important to me that I not be associated with, nor be involved with, any organized religion. In my mind I had all that my spirit needed: proof of the existence of God and that Jesus was my Savior. What could be more important than that? The answer to this question came to me about 22 years later.

In the years that followed my experience on Kodiak Island, I pursued my interests in life, still seeking all the pleasures the world had to offer. The near-death experience produced little or no changes in me. My relationship with God was on my terms. I had a nice little box wrapped with pretty ribbons into which I put God, limiting Him to the scope of my feeble mind and imagination. I would go to Him only when I was overwhelmed and had nowhere else to turn. There was no doubt in my mind that He existed, but I sought Him only when I thought I needed Him as I continued my pursuit of the pleasures offered by the world.

Upon returning home from Alaska, I finished college, eventually obtaining a master's degree. Shortly after that I was hired by a British company that sent me to the Philippines, where I lived and worked for one year performing embryo transfer procedures with cattle. After that I started my own embryo transfer business utilizing my family's ranch in the mountains of Colorado. Two years later I married my college sweetheart.

All this time I had what I thought was a great one-on-one

relationship with God; He was like an invisible friend who was willing to listen whenever I took the time to talk to Him. I didn't think that there was any need to study Scripture or fellowship with other believers. In fact, I was becoming more and more full of myself as I believed I was very special in God's sight since He revealed to me proof of His existence. I thought I had all that I needed in life and was content. Boy, was I wrong.

There were many extraordinary things that happened to me during the post near-death experience period of my life. Once while flying in a helicopter to the drilling rig in Alaska we encountered a serious wind shear that thrust us high up into the air. The propellers stopped turning, the bright red re-arm lights started flashing, and we started to fall to the ground. This time I knew I was going to die. My heart was pounding so hard I could see my chest move with every beat. My whole life flashed before my eyes as though I were watching it on a big screen in a movie theater. I saw things from my childhood that I had totally forgotten about. In my ignorance of the truth of life, I started praying to God, hoping that He would see that I had done enough good in my life to counter the bad so that I would be accepted into heaven.

Fortunately, Mike the chopper pilot was very experienced from the countless missions he flew in Vietnam. He kept his cool and persisted with working the controls as we were falling. Eventually the propellers started turning again, and Mike gained control of the helicopter, and we stopped falling. There was dead silence in the chopper for the rest of the trip to the drilling site.

Just before we landed, Mike spoke to us through the headsets and said, "In all my years of flying, that was the second time I ever encountered wind shear. If it was blowing down instead of up we'd all be spots on the rocks right now."

Death was knocking on the door in another incident with the helicopter. One day while on the way to work at the drilling site, we were flying low to the ground and fast. Usually we liked to fly higher up so we could look for grizzly bears. But for some reason on this day we didn't. After about 20 minutes into the flight I heard a loud thump behind me. Suddenly black smoke filled the cabin. Mike set the chopper down immediately. It turns out that a belt that turns a fan that cools the engine oil broke, and the engine started to burn oil. If we had been flying higher in the sky like usual we would have never made it to the ground without crashing. It was a very long walk back to camp that night!

Another scrape with death occurred as a result of a phone call that I received at 4:30 one morning. I was living at my parents' home right after I graduated from graduate school. With no job, and oh so poor, I had nowhere else to go. In order to raise money to make the trip home from college, I sold the puppies that my yellow Labrador retriever gave birth to a couple months earlier, the result of an unplanned pregnancy. After making a brief stop in Denver to post my name on the "Seeking Employment" bulletin board at a meeting of the International Embryo Transfer Society, I made my way home.

I answered the phone with my usual gravelly morning voice. "Hello?"

The voice on the other line had a heavy British accent. "Hello. Is a Mr. Jeff Eichhorn there?"

"Yeah, this is me," I replied, still trying to wake up.

"Oh, hello, Mr. Eichhorn," said the British voice. "This is Peter Bering calling from Oxfordshire, England. Do you still do embryo transfer in cattle?"

"Yeah," I replied, considerably more awake.

"How would you like to go to the Philippines?" he asked.

"Sure!" I replied enthusiastically.

Someone from the British company that Mr. Bering operated was at the meeting in Denver and saw my name on the bulletin board. Two weeks after the phone call, I was on a plane to England to meet with scientists there, and then I was off to the Philippines.

While in the Philippines working for a British company called International Embryos, Inc., I was held captive by a band of NPA (New People's Army) communist rebels near Gua Gua Pampanga. They thought I was a CIA agent! It all started when I became good friends with Ray Manlulu, one of the Filipinos who did graphic art work for the company that I worked for, and he invited me to go with him to his home in the province of Gua Gua Pampanga to meet his family and to experience the Ati Ati Han festival. It sounded like a great opportunity to immerse myself into Filipino culture, so I gladly accepted his invitation.

As I understand the meaning behind the Ati Ati Han, it is an ancient celebration that was originally started by tribal people to promote a festive atmosphere in order to drive away evil spirits. I compare today's Ati Ati Han celebrations to that of America's Thanksgiving of modern times, more or less used as an opportunity for family and friends to gather together and share a huge meal.

The morning of the festival was a typical intensely hot

and humid day in the Philippines. People were lined along the streets of Gua Gua for the big parade. As a group of teenage girls who were dancing in the parade passed by me, one of the girls ran over and grabbed my hand. Ray informed me that she wanted me to go join with her friends to dance the ritual Ati Ati Han. My first reaction was no way did I want to make a spectacle of myself in front of all those people! But as I looked around me, being the only white person present, I realized that it really didn't matter if I made a fool of myself in front of these people. And besides, earlier experiences with Filipinos had taught me that they are a giving and generous people, but they feel a great sense of shame whenever a guest like me rejects their offers. So I let the girl lead me to the center of the street and joined in the dance.

As I fumbled through the steps and hops of the dance, spectators pointed and laughed, exposing their wide and beautiful Filipino smiles. Little children ran up to me and gave me pieces of candy. When I popped a piece of candy into my mouth given to me by one little boy, he ran back hooting and jumping in the air as if something great had just happened. I quickly decided that my previous inhibitions of joining in the dance were unwarranted as the joy and fun of a white guy dancing the Ati Ati Han was wonderful for all to see.

Out of nowhere came the largest Filipino I had ever seen. He must have been at least six and a half feet tall weighing around 250 pounds. For some reason he followed me everywhere while dancing, with a bottle of rum in his hands. Every so often he would offer me a swig from his bottle. Hmm, I really did not want alcohol in my body in that

44

extreme heat, but I especially did not want to make this giant Filipino feel ashamed! So I placed my tongue over the top of the bottle as I went through the motions of taking a swig, being careful not to swallow any rum. The giant Filipino was delighted to have me share in his gift!

When the parade was over we went to Ray's auntie's house for a feast of all feasts. In all my life I have never seen so much food and so many different types of food all in one place! Table after table were covered with dishes, some of which were complete mysteries to me.

As I walked along the tables, various Filipina ladies piled food upon food on my plate, saying, "Sir Jeff, you must try this!" Of course it was one of the most flavorful meals I had ever eaten. The women kept coaxing me to eat and eat. Finally I reached a point where I snapped at one woman and said "No! I can't eat another bite!" Immediately her entire face burst into one infectious smile as she said, "Ah! Sir Jeff is finally full!" and snickered as she walked away.

The moment came when the meal was over, and I slumped back in my chair, so stuffed I could hardly move. Breathing was difficult as my stomach was so full there was little room for my diaphragm to expand. Just when I found a position in which I could relax and focus on digesting, a group of soldiers dressed in military fatigues and carrying M-16 rifles and machine guns entered the patio. Twenty or so soldiers formed a circle around the area. Then two men walked through the circle. One dressed in civilian clothes sat next to me on my left; the other, wearing a highly decorated military uniform, sat on my right.

The man in civilian clothes introduced himself and said in Filipino-accented English, "Sir Jeff, we seldom see white people in this area and we were wondering if you would mind if we ask you a few questions."

"No, I don't mind, ask me anything you want," I replied.

Then he introduced the man sitting to my right as the leader of that particular band of NPA. As if on cue, the leader spoke. "Sir Jeff, we wanted to know if you are CIA."

I laughed at the thought of me working for the CIA and replied, "If by CIA you mean the Central Intelligence Agency, the answer is no, I have never worked for any branch of the United States government in all my life."

Unsatisfied by my response, the leader took from his pocket a metal object about eight inches long and a half inch wide. The object was laden with beautiful gemstones of different brilliant colors. He displayed the object where I could clearly see the intricate interlay of gemstones. When he pressed one of the gemstones, two blades instantly protruded from each end of the object. As he spun the object around in circles with his fingertips, he proudly informed me that this was a bulacan knife that he had used to slit the throats of many men. He then held the knife so that the blades would pass under my chin as they twirled around in circles held by his fingertips. Then he asked me pointblank, "Sir Jeff, are you a CIA agent?"

This was getting quite serious. The heat had made me perspire profusely all day, but now my sweat was emanating copiously from pure nervousness. I knew my best option was to remain calm, if possible.

Holding my head completely still I gave a blunt reply. *"No!"*

In an attempt to change the subject, I commented on

the beauty of the knife's handle and that he had amazing dexterity in his fingers to be able to handle the knife in the manner in which he was.

The leader persisted and asked again if I worked for the CIA. Again I said a resounding *No!* and followed with an explanation that there are both good and bad things about my government, about how the American people are basically good people, but sometimes we elect politicians who get carried away with the power they have in certain positions of government. I started rambling on with a dissertation regarding my opinions of the American government, not because I thought the man holding the knife was interested in what I had to say, but because talking produced a calming effect in me from knowing that as long as I heard my own voice, my throat had not yet been slit.

My oratory rambling was interrupted by the man dressed in civilian clothes. He explained to me that whenever they see a white man in this area they assume there is a good chance he works for the CIA. The CIA had been a problem for them in their quest to overtake the government of the Philippines. They were fed up with the extreme poverty in which the majority of Filipinos live, while corruption runs rampant as their politicians hoard the wealth of their country. The US government was paying hundreds of millions of dollars to the Philippine government for rent for its military bases there. Filipino government officials were using the money to live in extravagance while repressing the poor. And these men who surrounded me blamed my government in part for their problems and had taken up arms in an attempt to rectify the situation.

Strangely enough, as this man was talking, I began to feel

some empathy for these guys as they reminded me of how the civilian population of America took up arms to fight British repression back in the colonial days of America. If I was not a CIA agent, then he wanted to know why I was there.

Good question, I thought. *It will give me a chance to talk awhile longer.* So I explained, as the leader continued to periodically swipe the knife blades beneath my chin, that I had been hired by a British company and sent to the Philippines to perform embryo transfer procedures with the cattle here. I took my time in explaining how this work would help their beef production, which should add much needed protein into the diets of the Filipinos.

Time seemed to stand still as I was being questioned over and over, and with each answer I tried to drag out my response to be as long as possible. Then I spoke of how I met and befriended Ray, who had invited me to Gua Gua to meet his family and experience the Ati Ati Han celebration.

Ray interrupted me and stood up as he spoke to verify my story. He was emphatic as he declared that I was telling the truth. When Ray finished speaking, the leader put down the knife. He lowered his head as if he were deep in contemplation. Just then the giant Filipino who had followed me around during the parade appeared.

He said with heavily accented English, "I followed Sir Jeff all around town today. He danced the Ati Ati Han with our daughters, he accepts the gifts of candy from our children, he drinks rum from my bottle. I believe him!"

Some of the soldiers who were standing around us began to speak up. "I believe him!" said one. "I believe him!" said another and another.

And then there was a moment of silence. All eyes gazed

upon the leader. The silence was so loud it was deafening to my ears. Ever so slowly the leader raised his head and, after egging on the silence for a moment or two longer, he raised his hand and declared, "I believe him!"

A cheer arose from all those present. The leader turned to me and hugged me and kissed me on both cheeks. He told me that he loved the American people but could not stand our government. I laughed (it was just the moment I needed to release pent-up nervousness) and replied that many Americans feel the same way. Then he stretched his hand way up in the air and snapped his fingers several times.

Soon two Filipinos arrived carrying what looked to be a ten-gallon jar of beer and a large bottle of rum. From somewhere, the man in civilian clothes produced a small glass. The mood on the patio became festive as he filled the glass half with rum and half with beer and handed it to the leader. With the glass raised, the leader gave a toast to the people of our two countries and then chugged down the entire contents of the glass with a single motion. Then the glass was refilled and it was my turn. I thought, *Here I go again,* but this time I would be unable to fake it. Not wanting to insult these guys in any way, I followed suit with the leader and chugged.

The half-rum half-beer concoction was passed around to everyone present, one at a time. All the while the leader and the civilian eagerly explained their plight. They even invited me to visit their camp in the jungle. I gracefully declined their offer, making the excuse that I had to get back to work on the island of Negros, thinking the less I knew of them the better. This went on until all of the rum and beer was consumed.

And then, seemingly all of a sudden, I looked around and saw that everyone was lying on the ground passed out, right where they were standing! The two guys sitting next to me had their heads resting on their arms on the table and were fast asleep! I shook Ray and with a loud whisper in his ear I said, "Hey! Wake up! We gotta get out of here!" Then we sped away on his moped.

There were several other close encounters with death that I experienced while living and working on my family's ranch way up in the mountains of Colorado, upon my return home from the Philippines. One time when I was riding my horse Rusty deep into the West Elk Wilderness looking for stray cattle, Rusty lost his footing on a steep hillside. He rolled over the top of me as we were tumbling down the rocky hillside. I have no idea how Rusty and I escaped that without serious injury or death.

In another incident on the ranch, I drove our old Massey Ferguson tractor to the top of "Suicide Hill" with a load of fence posts. I needed to build a stretch of fence along the creek below, and I thought it would be much easier to roll the posts down the hill rather than carry them across the creek. As I carefully drove the tractor to the edge of the top of the hill, the ground gave way, and I started heading straight down the steep slope of Suicide Hill. The tractor hit a rock, which sent it tumbling head over heels and bucked me off like a bronco! I was flying through the air head-first, straight out in front of the path of the tractor.

In the split second that I had time to think, I figured I should tuck my shoulder and roll the instant I hit the ground to try to get out of the path of the tumbling tractor. When I hit the ground rolling, my hat fell off my head at the very spot where my head hit the ground. In the next instant I saw the tractor smash my hat, then bounce up in the air as it tumbled end-over-end down to the bottom.

All of these scrapes with death occurred after the drowning incident on Kodiak Island. An earlier incident occurred in high school when I broke my neck while making a tackle in a varsity football game. The third cervical vertebra was fractured, and a spinal process bone was completely broken. According to the doctor who looked at the 50 or so x-rays taken of my neck, if the fracture of the vertebra had occurred about one-eighth of an inch farther up or down, I would either be dead or paralyzed for life.

I mention these flirts with death because they were very important in how my psyche developed over time. Through these experiences I became enamored with myself. Because I had escaped the grasp of death so many times, I began to feel that I was invincible and indestructible. *God must have some great purpose for my life since He has saved me so many times,* I thought. I was so wrapped up in myself that I neglected to be thankful to God for all He had done for me. It was as if God had been trying to get my attention through all the crazy experiences, but for some reason I wouldn't listen.

The experiences in my life up to this point gave me the confidence to believe that I could take care of myself without any help, even from God. Despite the fact that I was beginning to believe that God had kept me alive for some great unknown purpose, I pretty much went my own way and was quite full of myself. My pride and ego were bulging to the point where there was little room left for God. Perhaps God was setting me up for what was yet to come...

Trial And Tribulation

Such was the status of my spirituality at the time I married my college sweetheart. My faith in the existence of God was strong, but my knowledge and understanding of God were very weak. Upon returning home from the Philippines, my family and I got together and decided to pool our resources to rejuvenate our family ranch, and I started my own embryo transfer business. It was because of this that I became reunited with my long lost sweetheart from college.

After we graduated from undergraduate school, my sweetheart and I lost touch with each other. Then on one summer day in 1989 she stepped out of her truck and onto my family's ranch. She was just passing through the area during a cross-country move, and through mutual friends it was decided that we should have a little reunion at my family's ranch. It had been nine years since I last saw her. She was beautiful!

When I saw her working with a testy horse of mine, I thought that she would make a good wife to a rancher. Living a solitary life way up in the mountains had its benefits for me, but it also included times of intense loneliness. I wanted to share this life with someone, and it made complete sense to me that God had planned for us to be together. We married the following spring.

The birth of our first baby was very traumatic. I had a good rapport with the physician, so he allowed me into the surgery room for an emergency C-section. I watched in horror as the lives of both mother and baby were nearly lost. My wife had to receive a general anesthetic prior to recovering the baby from her womb because the local anesthetic wasn't working, as she could feel the incisions being made to her stomach. This meant there was little time to rescue the baby. After a few very tense moments, the baby arrived; it was the most brilliant blue color I have ever seen. The baby was obviously affected by the anesthesia and lack of oxygen. Immediately the lead surgeon cried out to the anesthesiologist to assist with the baby. He had to deny the surgeon's request as he was struggling to prevent my wife from swallowing her tongue. And so there I was, watching the lead surgeon in helpless desperation as he held my blue baby, and the anesthesiologist was frantically trying to save my wife's life, while the assistant surgeon was trying to stuff her insides back inside. I thought for sure I was going to lose them both.

But everything worked out fine in the end. My baby was the most beautiful creature in the entire world. The doctors gave me the task of holding the oxygen hose to her nose while the rest of crew worked on my wife. Eventually the vibrant blue color of her skin turned pink. As I held her for the first time I realized that she was the reason God kept me alive all these years. My purpose for living was to take care of this baby and shower her with love. I held her in my arms tight to my chest and gave her the first drink of milk, as her mother was in the recovery room. The nurses didn't get to hold my baby until I had fallen asleep in a chair with the baby clutched in my arms.

Two years later our second daughter was born via another emergency C-section. She was born in a different hospital, and this time they would not allow me into the surgery room. After an eternity of pacing up and down the hallways of the hospital, a nurse finally emerged from the surgery room to present to me my second daughter. She was so beautiful! Her cheeks were a glowing red color like a rose. As I held her in my arms I promised her that I would always love her and be there for her. God had given me a second purpose for my life.

I had it all, a beautiful wife, two beautiful daughters, and a strong faith in God. As the girls were growing up, we started attending various churches periodically as their mother and I thought it would be good for the girls. Though we struggled financially, I was content. However, our financial struggle began to take its toll on my wife.

As my wife and I began to focus much of our energy on our respective businesses to try and make ends meet, we began to grow apart. The children became the focus of our marriage rather than each other. Though we attended church on a semi-regular basis, we did not seek help from God for our marital problems. Several attempts to resolve our differences with various "marriage counselors" failed. The problems we had were not the problem — how we dealt with the problems was the problem. And I for one failed miserably with how I dealt with the problems. My wife had had enough of me and my struggling-to-survive lifestyle, and it was time for her to move on.

Toward the end of our last counseling sessions, the discussions changed from what was needed to be done to save the marriage to what was the best way to end the marriage, especially with concern for the children. In no way did I ever believe that divorce would be an option. My denial that there were serious problems in the marriage that could lead to divorce was one of the problems that led to the divorce. After all, there was no abuse of any kind, no adulterous affairs, or anything like that; to me we simply had problems with getting along that were hampered by financial difficulties. I thought we just needed a little more time — more time for my business to grow and resolve some of the financial stress, more time for us to pass through this middle phase of our lives. The reality of divorce hit me like a brick. I was devastated.

I began to pray in earnest to God. Pouring out my heart to God I asked Him to heal our marriage, to soften my wife's heart. Over and over I asked God to change what was happening to our marriage, to change this and change that, but no change occurred. Why was He forsaking me? Then one day in April, while taking communion in church, my life was changed forever.

As I pushed the bread of communion into my mouth, for the first time in my life I began to ask God to change me. With all my heart I cried out to God to change me. Then I felt a shock of electricity hit the back of my neck where my head attaches to my spinal column. I mean this was a real jolt!

Often in church I would feel all tingly inside or get goose bumps while singing songs or sometimes in response to a good sermon. But this electric shock was totally different. It was like someone had touched me with a power cord. I felt a sting spread throughout my entire body. None of my previous bouts with death were enough to grab my attention, but this bolt of electricity that struck me from out of nowhere nearly knocked me out of my chair! Little did I know it at the time, but I would never be the same again. God *finally* got my attention!

The next day I had to flush a cow for embryos. During the flush I began to see images in my mind of stupid things I had said or done that caused harm to my marriage and to my wife. While my arm was inside the cow, tears flowed from my eyes as I realized what a jerk I had been at times. For the first time in my life I began to take a close look at myself objectively, and I didn't like what I saw. I realized that I had a lot of anger pent up inside me. Sometimes this anger would push its way to the surface, and I would react to little instances with more gusto than was appropriate. It's as if that jolt of electricity that I experienced the day before had zapped away whatever it was that prevented me from seeing myself for who I was instead of who I wanted to be.

There were certain news and talk-show stations on the radio that I used to listen to whenever possible. I could not listen to them anymore because when I did I could feel the anger building up inside me — anger at politicians, anger at the world, and eventually, anger at myself. The ugly process of self-realization began to grow. There were many things I saw that I didn't like about J. Martin Eichhorn. It was always so easy to see the faults in other people; now I was finally beginning to see the faults in myself.

As each day proceeded, the images of my own contributions to the failure of my marriage increased. So many things appeared in my mind that I wished I could somehow change. I told my wife about these things and how I had changed deep down inside. I even wrote to her in a letter how I believed I had been touched by the Holy Spirit while taking communion in church, which gave me the gift of seeing myself objectively. I asked for her forgiveness and reconciliation. But it was too little too late; she had already made up her mind. We divorced when the children were ages 11 and 13.

Transformation

The divorce was by far the most devastatingly painful experience of my life. Not even a broken neck could compare in intensity of pain. I did not want the divorce, but there was nothing I could do to stop it. Depression set in like a persistent offensive odor. It ruined everything. My joy of living was gone. I couldn't stand coming home to an empty house. The stench of loneliness permeated the air around me, and I couldn't seem to get rid of it. Even when with my true and trusted friends, I still felt all alone.

My part in the failure of the marriage was hard enough to deal with, but not seeing my daughters every day was unbearable. Not a single day would pass without me crying until there were no tears left. Often while driving home after dropping the girls off at their mom's house, I had to pull the car over to the side of the road because I was crying so hard I couldn't see. I was a totally broken man.

As word of the divorce spread throughout the congregation of the church we occasionally attended, some very strange things began to happen. Men whom I barely knew came up to me and hugged me (and I was not used to being hugged by men!) and prayed for my family and me. Once, while waiting for my car to get a change of oil, I sat in the waiting room fighting back tears as I was drenched in doom and gloom. An acquaintance from church walked in and saw me, and right then and there in the parts department of the Ford dealership he put his arm on my shoulder and prayed over me. It was just what I needed to get through that day. The sincerity of these men from the church I attended impressed me. I was not used to being showered with so much love from men I hardly knew.

Each day was a struggle. I was tempted with many things, but the greatest of these was the desire to sell everything I owned and move far away. Daily reminders of the divorce and not being able to hug my children each and every day perpetuated my depression. But I knew I couldn't leave my girls. Just when I thought I was going to break, something would happen to get me through the day. Sometimes it would be a simple e-mail with a Bible verse from an acquaintance at church, or a phone call from someone who was just checking in.

In order to avoid going home to my empty house, I became involved with several activities at church. For the first time in my life I felt drawn to church. The sincere love that I felt from many people during the time of my greatest need was captivating. I became a leader with the youth group, meeting with high school kids on Wednesday nights, and I formed a small group where I met with four teenage boys on Monday nights. Hey! I gave up Monday Night Football to meet with my guys!

That experience with those kids taught me so much. It

was the beginning of my making sacrifices in my life in service to others. For the first time I began to get a glimpse of what it means to be fulfilled.

But I needed more. I decided to join Men's Fraternity, a 26-week session by Dr. Robert M. Lewis on "The Quest for Authentic Manhood," which met on Tuesday nights. This course was exactly what I needed to begin healing the wounds of divorce. The first half of the course opened up my eyes to see why I was the way I was. It helped me to understand that I was deprived of God in my daily life and to comprehend the mistakes I made in my marriage. My previous experience with being touched by the Holy Spirit while taking communion prepared me for getting the most out of this part of the course. I was ready for a deep comprehensive look into the innermost me.

With the first half of the course being an exercise to sort of break a man down (which I was already), the second half focused on building him back up to be the man God created him to be. Throughout the course Dr. Lewis referred to Scripture as the textbook for his teaching. I was astonished to discover that all the things I was dealing with throughout my life were written about in the Bible! A burning hunger to know Jesus and His teachings grew in my mind as well as in my heart. It developed into a voracious appetite for Christ. A dear couple who were witnessing my transformation gave me a study Bible in a version that I could understand. It instantly became my favorite book.

One of the ways I discovered that I could satisfy my appetite for Christ was through my relationships with my Christian brothers. Some of these men I first met through the Men's Fraternity course. I've never been one who liked to talk about my feelings and problems with others. But I discovered a great healing occurs whenever I open up to these men, and by exposing our hearts to each other we are also sharing the burdens of this life with one another, developing bonds that will last a lifetime. These men hold me accountable to my commitment to Christ, and I them. So, with church on Sundays, small group on Mondays, Men's Fraternity on Tuesdays, and High School Youth Group on Wednesdays, I was beginning to develop a way to get through each week, let alone each day. My demeanor gradually began to improve.

And then Jeanette came into my life. She had been in a car accident that left her paralyzed and confined to a wheelchair. She had two small boys, and her husband had left her and the boys after the accident. And she needed help with things around her house and yard. Another youth group leader and I took some teenagers to her house to perform odd jobs such as cleaning the gutters, picking up trash, washing windows, spraying the exterior of the house, etc., on one Saturday. Shortly after that I enlisted the help of men from Men's Fraternity to perform other work at Jeanette's, such as removing the carpet so she could get around the house in her wheelchair more easily, along with other home repairs.

A defining moment in my life came one night as I was leaving Jeanette's after an evening of pulling up carpet. As I was about to walk out the door, Jeanette started to thank me over and over for the work we were doing. I put my hand on her shoulder and told her to thank Jesus Christ, as it was His love working through us that was the reason we were there. Jeanette smiled and told me that she thanked Jesus every day for the blessings He had given to her. Then she started talking about how blessed she felt from the accident. She recounted the long days in the hospital and all the cards she received from family and friends, each one wishing God's blessing on her. Eventually she realized how much God loved her, and she said she would never have come to that realization without the car accident that left her bound to a wheelchair.

I was flabbergasted. Tears oozed from my eyes as I was walking out to my car. Here was this woman praising God, considering herself to be blessed by her paralysis, because it brought her closer to Him. Wow! All this time I had been feeling sorry for myself for going through the divorce, showering myself with self-pity. I walked away from Jeanette's that night not only feeling ashamed of myself but also feeling hopeful that if Jeanette could overcome her circumstances then surely so could I. As if a stack of bricks just hit me in the head, I came to the realization that my situation was not nearly as bad as I made it out to be. It is truly amazing how God often brings someone into our lives to touch us with His love. I will never forget Jeanette or that night!

Two summers after I completed the Men's Fraternity course I went back to Alaska. As part of that trip I took a four-day solo backpack trip far up the East Fork of the Toklat River in Denali National Park. It was in the heart of grizzly bear and wolf country. Even though I was by myself, I was not alone. A sow grizzly and her two cubs entertained me for several hours at the start of my trek. The baby cubs engaged in a boxing match in a pond along the trail I was to follow. I had no choice but to hide in the bushes and watch until Momma Griz decided it was time to amble on to another berry patch somewhere up the canyon.

Later on I had an indescribable connection to a lone bull caribou that was grazing on the tundra. The caribou, with his majestic horns, allowed me to get very close to him. In fact, he did not seem the least bit bothered by my presence. He just went about his business, grazing with periodic glances in my direction. I felt a strange sort of connection to that animal, like we were two males of our respective species sharing the same time and space in a playground that only God could create. I also felt the presence of God the whole time. Perhaps God was using the caribou to let me know He was there. For the first time in three years I realized that there really was life after divorce, and it would be what I make of it.

Three months later, the church I was attending sent me on a mission trip to Spain. Our task was to construct a building for a full-time missionary whom the church supported. I found myself inspired by doing the work of the Lord, producing in me a craving to do more.

Then I found out about Charisma Bethel Children's Home (CBCH), an orphanage on the southern island of Mindanao in the Philippines. I can't explain why or how, but I felt drawn to the orphans even though I had not yet met them. My daughters and I went to various discount stores and purchased Christmas gifts for each of the 57 orphans, and mailed them to the Philippines.

My idea was to visit the orphans after they received the gifts and talk to them about the love of Jesus — that He loved them so much, He put it on the heart of a guy on the other side of the world to send the gifts. I thought I could somehow be a blessing to them, that maybe I could bring them hope by telling them that someone out there in the world whom they had never met loved them very much. Ha! When I went to the Philippines to visit the orphans, they showered me with so much love that I was the one who was blessed. I did not give my talk because I was so taken by the fact that they had so little yet showed so much love. It was obvious to me that they knew more about the love of Christ than I did. Never before in my life had I been around any group of people who were as filled with the Holy Spirit as these children. The orphans were the ones who gave *me* hope!

Shortly after this visit to CBCH, a landslide occurred that just missed their home. On my second visit to the orphanage, my heart sank as I stood on the spot where I could see the devastation of the landslide through the jungle and how it had just missed the orphanage. At that moment in time God put it on my heart to try to do something for these kids. It made no sense to me whatsoever why God would put it on my heart to help these kids; after all, I was just a poor cattle rancher struggling to make ends meet. What could I do?

Well, as it turns out, God was able to use me, just an ordinary person, to do something rather extraordinary. All I needed to do was be obedient. Upon returning home from the second visit to the orphanage I talked with my Christian brother Shane, who had visited the orphanage with me on the first trip, about their situation.

I grabbed a hold of Shane's shoulders and started shaking him as I yelled, "We gotta do something, man! We gotta help those kids!"

Shane yelled back, "I know, I know! Just let go of me!"

Shane was as fired up as I to help, and we teamed up with a local Filipina, Luz, to brainstorm and produce a fund-raising event. Completely inexperienced with fund-raising but submissive to God's will and immersed in prayer, our efforts produced over $50,000 and counting! The new home for the orphans, called *Atlantis*, is near completion, and hopefully soon we will be moving on to construction of more buildings for homeless children and raising funds to provide them with a college education.

My experiences with the orphanage — doing something that I received no direct benefit from — was the medicine that healed the wounds of divorce. My joy of living not only returned but was multiplied beyond belief because now I had a purpose in life that went beyond me.

God rewarded my obedience to His call by bringing Tata into my life. I met Tata through my visits to the orphanage. She is a Filipina who worked in the town near the orphanage, and she is the one who first introduced me to CBCH. We are now happily married, and my relationship with her has enlightened me as to what the Bible refers to about how the two (man and wife) shall become one.

Renewing
Of The Mind

As I look back over my life, I see myself as the caterpillars that I observed in my youth as they transformed from creepy-looking crawling creatures to beautiful creatures of flight. I realize now that I allowed the influence of the world to weave a web of cocoon around me; I was trapped in the confines of self-gratification and the pursuit of treasure offered by the world. My life was all about me pursuing and capturing what I wanted. And along with it came despair, worry, sorrow, and the emptiness of failure.

Blinded by a veil of self-indulgence, I could not see past my outstretched hand. I was strong, seemingly invincible, and quite full of myself. The cocoon of the world that I was entrapped in was collapsing around me, strangling me of pure joy and love, yet once deceiving me into believing that I had all that I needed in life to be happy. And isn't that what the world teaches us? That our primary goal in this life is to be happy? The problem is in what the world tells us we need to have or to be in order to know happiness.

Struggling to break out of my cocoon, I was hopeless. It wasn't until I was humbled by being totally and unequivocally broken by the heartbreak of divorce before I could admit that I couldn't continue on my own — I needed help. My pride and ego had prevented me from escaping the cocoon. I had to be in a state of mind where I had nowhere and no one else to turn to except God and Jesus Christ.

During my period of self-examination I discovered that I was striving to become the person I wanted to be. At first it was sports and then it was the life of a cattle rancher that captured the focus of my existence. There is nothing wrong with those pursuits in life in and of themselves, except that I was the end and the means of the pursuit and left God out.

Change didn't occur until I was humbled to the point where I was willing to let go of who I wanted to be and living life for myself. Then I was able to open up to God and ask Him to change me. At that precise moment in time, when the jolt of electricity zapped the back of my neck, I was able to break through the confinement of the cocoon I had woven around myself and begin the process of becoming the man God created me to be. It took having more than just a casual understanding of who God really is, which in turn gave me much greater fulfillment in being a cattle rancher and sports enthusiast.

Once I started reading Scripture, I discovered how so much of my life was foretold in its pages. Romans 12:2 sums it up best; *Do not conform any longer to the pattern of this world, but be transformed by the renewing of your mind. Then you will be able to test and approve what God's will is – his good, pleasing and perfect will.*

It's as if Jesus was speaking to me when He said these words as recorded by Matthew in chapter 10 of his gospel, verse 39; *Whoever finds his life will lose it, and whoever loses his life for my sake will find it.* I was stuck in the trap of finding my place in this world, and it wasn't until I gave it up to seek my place in the kingdom of God that I realized complete peace and joy in knowing who I am in Christ.

The renewing of my mind has brought out of me a whole new outlook and attitude toward life. One such example is related to my work as an embryologist. The "old" me used to think, with my nose high in the air as I was walking down to the corrals to flush a cow for embryos, *Here goes the world-class embryologist going down to flush another cow.* The new me goes to the floor on my knees before every flush and says a prayer to God in thanksgiving for the ability He has given me to earn a living from flushing cows.

Another example is that I used to think I was happy and content with *my* family, *my* land, *my* cows, *my* horses, and *my* life. I would fight to no end to keep these things in my possession. Now I have the joy and fulfillment of knowing that the things in my possession are God's gifts to me as a steward of a piece of His creation. If someday I were to lose these things in my possession, I would still have left the joy and contentment that only a relationship with Christ can bring to one's soul. In other words, no longer is my joy and contentment in life related to the things that I have or to what I do for a living. This realization has really opened up a bright new world for me.

Perhaps the best example of the benefits of my mind renewed has to do with my mom. I loved Mom with all my heart. While growing up I hated to think of the time when she would die. Luckily for me she passed away after I was transformed and had proof of life that lies beyond this life. This spiritual enlightenment enabled me to give a eulogy at her funeral service without breaking down. There was no way I could have done that before. Sure I grieved for her after her passing. But I also rejoice in knowing where she is now. I was able to get through all this because I no longer fear death.

Indeed, I can verify that once my mind was renewed it became clear what God's good and pleasing will for my life was. In 2004, I founded the Hands On Foundation. Our involvement with the orphanage in the Philippines can attest to God's will for this phase of my life. There is no way I would have ever become involved with this type of work before the renewing of my mind. Now God's will for my life is quite clear, and I have experienced more pure joy since being involved with the orphans of *Atlantis* than I ever thought was possible.

Witnessing those children pour out their hearts to God in praise and worship is indeed a humbling experience. To see that much joy coming from children who have had terrible things happen to them in their young lives is a testimony to the awesome power and love of Jesus Christ. A teen from Montrose, Colorado, who visited the orphans with me in the summer of 2008, commented: *These are the happiest people I have ever seen.* From her experience with the orphans, another teen said, *There is going to be a great reunion in heaven some day!* The orphans of *Atlantis* exude a tremendous joy of living and have a great hope for the future because of the Word of God that is taught to them on a daily basis by the amazing people who take care of them. Oh! If only we all could fill our hearts with the love of Christ like that!

In his book, *90 Minutes In Heaven*, Don Piper tells the remarkable story of when he died, experienced heaven, and returned to his earthly body. He was in a terrible car accident that killed him. Paramedics who arrived at the scene checked his vital signs and pronounced him dead and then went on to take care of the other accident victims. A minister who was stuck in the ensuing traffic offered his assistance. He questioned the paramedics about the condition of the person in Don's car; they responded by telling him that the driver was dead. Feeling drawn to the car, the minister reached into Don's smashed car and touched his mangled body and prayed. Soon afterward, Don's spirit returned to his body along with his pulse.

Don's description of what he experienced during the 90 minutes in which he was dead and visited heaven is extraordinary to say the least. Both Don and I have trouble coming up with the right words to explain our respective experiences. But some of Don's descriptive phrases express more precisely what I experienced than do my own words. He saw light *with a brilliance beyond earthly comprehension or description* with *vivid dazzling colors*. As he explains, it was as if he had a glimpse into another dimension and felt *love beyond belief* and that he had a tremendous feeling of being home with no worries, anxieties, concerns, or needs, and that time had no meaning. He experienced feelings of perfect joy and peacefulness and was *deliriously happy*. One particular statement he makes that describes precisely what I felt was that he *had a heightened awareness of Jesus* and that he *knew without being aware of how* he *had absorbed that information.* Another striking aspect of Don's experience was that he saw with perfect clarity many friends and relatives who had died before him, similar to what happened to me when I saw Granny's face while drowning.

As Don points out in his book, a scientific study on near-death experiences was conducted in the Netherlands in 2001, and reported in the journal of the British Medical Society, *Lancet*. This study involved hundreds of patients who had been resuscitated after their hearts failed and were considered to be clinically dead. From interviews of the patients who reported having recollections during the time that they were clinically dead, the researchers concluded that these after-death experiences are *something we would all desperately like to believe to be true*. This may explain some or many reports of such experiences, and may even explain part of my own experience. However, there is one important exception to my experience that does not fit the conclusion of the Netherlands study. That is the role of Granny in my experience. Seeing her face in the tunnel of light while drowning, is certainly not something that I would have desperately wanted to see, even on the subconscious level, as my memories of her are not of fondness and joy.

Both Don and I feel a strong sense that there is a reason we are alive today. We share the desire that our stories will bring hope and encouragement to others in the knowledge that God truly exists, that death is not to be feared, and that Jesus really is the *Way, the Truth and the Life* (John 14:6). No matter what the skeptics may say, we both know that our experiences were real and that our lives have changed.

Reflections

Much of the change in me has been brought about through the realization that I am saved through faith by what Jesus did on the cross, not by adding up the good and bad things I've done in my life and hoping for the best. I used to believe that anyone who was a "good person" would make it into heaven. Now I realize that this manner of thinking diminishes what Jesus did. If we can be good enough to make it into heaven on our own accord then there was no need for God to be born into this world in the person of Jesus Christ. The change in me occurred once I got beyond just hearing the words "Jesus died for me" and began to fully realize what those words meant.

Most of us who knew Granny would probably not consider her to be a "good person," especially in her later years. She was quick to hurt others with words that stung the heart, and seemingly cared not about how hurtful her comments were to her family. But I am absolutely convinced that she is alive in heaven and that she was sent by God to check on me, for reasons only He knows. After many years of hindsight, I can only explain it by saying that as I was drowning my body and brain were starving for oxygen. My soul was on the verge of being released from the confines of my body. Being in this condition may have allowed my mind to perceive an open "door" to heaven and that which lies beyond this life. A brief connection was made between heaven and my spirit, and Granny was able to reach out to me in a way I can't understand. People who knew Granny when she was much younger have told me that she was a good Christian woman. Perhaps, then, it is true that being a "good person" is not a prerequisite for getting into heaven.

One of the lies of the world that I used to believe is that people are basically good. But is that really true? I know that if I acted on all the urges and impulses that naturally come upon me, then I would have been locked up in prison long ago. Fear and respect for the laws of the land are what have kept me out of trouble more so than anything else. Often when I am in a bank or at a store and I see a big wad of money behind the counter, my first thought is to grab the money and run. And sometimes if someone pulls out in front of me in traffic I feel like forcing the guy over to the side of the road to beat him to a pulp. I don't do it because I know what the consequences will be. But my basic instinct is to do wrong, not good.

If people are by nature basically good, then why does anarchy always result in violence and chaos? The resources exist to feed and clothe all of the people in the world. So if we are basically good people, then why is starvation still a huge problem in the world? How many basically good people ignore the homeless when they pass by them? And how much time do we, basically good people, spend doing good things only for the sake of doing good compared with the amount of time we spend taking care of our own desires? The lies that people are basically good and that basically good people will enter into heaven persist because it makes life easier to bear than dealing with the need for a savior. Perhaps truly good people can make their own way into the presence of God and heaven. As for me, I reject the notion that I have within me the power to do enough good in this world to warrant a pass into heaven. I choose to believe that I have a great need for a savior who has paid my debt to God for the sins I commit, and that savior is Jesus Christ.

I owe a great debt of gratitude to many Christian brothers and sisters whom I've entered into fellowship with. It is truly amazing to be part of a group of people who really care about one another. Often when I first meet someone who is sold out for Christ, we immediately develop a bond that surpasses understanding, even if we have nothing else in common. It's uncanny how many times this has happened since I've changed. I've learned how God uses these people to show His love for me and that their trust in God is infectious to the point where I can now quickly overcome the worry and feelings of despair that this world incessantly brings to my life.

Reading Scripture together and fellowshipping with others have taught me countless lessons about the difference between religion and having a personal relationship with Jesus. Before, I believed that being a Christian was synonymous with the rituals performed in a church. Now I realize what matters most is in knowing who I am in Christ. This awareness came to me by getting to know Jesus through the pages of Scripture and through fellowshipping with other believers, and especially through doing things in my life in obedience to the Word of God. Church is not the building or even the worship service and sermon, but it is the lives of people who dwell within.

The best advice I can give to new believers is to go out and do something! Help somebody in a way where you receive absolutely no benefit whatsoever. Worshiping and reading Scripture and fellowshipping with other believers are all good nourishment for the soul. But doing something good for someone simply for goodness sake, especially if it requires some sacrifice on your part, is the best way to learn and understand what the love of Christ is all about. For isn't that what Christ Himself was all about?

In the beginning of my life I had the childlike faith that Jesus talked about as reported in Mark 10:15; *I tell you the truth, anyone who will not receive the kingdom of God like a little child will never enter it.* I believed in Him without questioning or requiring proof gained through empirical research. But then, in response to matters going on in the world, I began to question and doubt the existence of God.

Inside my cocoon I fell into the trap that many of us fall prey to — the trap of searching for God through our physical senses. But as Jesus said in the Bible (John 4:24), *God is Spirit: and his worshipers must worship in spirit and in truth.* My problem was that I always tried to figure out the existence and nature of God by thinking through empirical evidence. I never realized that I was trying to use my perceptions and understanding of the physical world around me to make sense of the existence of a non-physical spiritual being. The near-death experience while drowning was my first contact with the purely spiritual reality. As my body was dying, my spirit was freed of the physical constraints of the body enough so that I could hear the voice calling me to Jesus, and see the light of heaven.

My search for the truth through philosophy led me exactly to where Paul warned the church at Colosse not to go. *See to it that no one takes you captive through hollow and deceptive philosophy, which depends on human tradition and the basic principles of this world rather than on Christ* (Colossians 2:8). I became captive in the cocoon made up of the fibers of worldly desires and human interpretation of life.

While in my cocoon I struggled for answers, just as Amos (8:11-13) predicted. *The days are coming, declares the Sovereign Lord, when I will send a famine through the land — not a famine of food or a thirst for water, but a famine of hearing the words of the Lord. Men will stagger from sea to sea and wander from north to east, searching for the word of the Lord, but they will not find it. In that day the lovely young women and strong young men will faint because of thirst.*

At one point in time I felt like I was forsaken by God because He did not save my marriage. It is clear to me now that I had to go through that suffering in order to be humbled to the point where I would allow Him to change me into the person He created me to be. After all, why should I expect to go through this life without serious pain and suffering when Jesus endured horrendous torture for my sake?

Jesus' explanation of the Parable of the Four Soils fits me perfectly (Luke 8:14); *The seed that fell among thorns stands for those who hear, but as they go on their way they are choked by life's worries, riches and pleasures, and they do not mature.* It wasn't until I was humbled enough to take a good hard look at myself that my heart was changed, and so, too, was the essence of my being such that, as Jesus continues in the next verse, *But the seed on good soil stands for those with a noble and good heart, who hear the word, retain it, and by persevering produce a crop.*

One of the most striking revelations that came to me while reading Scripture occurred the first time I read the Gospel of John. In chapter 8 verse 12 he says; *When Jesus spoke to the people, he said, 'I am the light of the world. Whoever follows me will never walk in darkness, but will have the light of life.'* I nearly fell out of my chair when I read this verse. Could the tunnel of light that I saw when I was drowning be the light of life Jesus talked about? It was as if the door of heaven had opened up, exposing a ray of the light of heaven through which Granny traveled to see me. Remember that I was completely unaware of this verse, or any other verses in Scripture for that matter, before the incident!

The relevance of Psalm 56 verse 13 to my experience while drowning is remarkable. *For you have delivered me from death and my feet from stumbling, that I may walk before God in the light of life.* There are many verses in Scripture that refer to God and Jesus and light, such as this verse from Isaiah 9:2: *The people walking in darkness have seen a great light; on those living in the land of the shadow of death a light has dawned.*

When Don Piper died, he saw a magnificent light but did not see a tunnel of light, nor did he hear a voice calling to him as I did. One explanation for this discrepancy may be that Don died instantly, and he immediately arrived at the gates of heaven because he was a true believer in Christ at the time of his death. Whereas I was merely on the verge of death, at which time I did not believe in the existence of God and only had a fleeting knowledge of Jesus Christ. Perhaps this is an indication that our life experiences, which form our individual perception of life after death, influence our experience of death.

My near-death experience taught me that when we die, we may be given the choice to follow the path that leads to Jesus. If we know Jesus and His love, and choose to follow Him in this life, then there may be no choice to make in death, as we are taken up into heaven or a heavenly place immediately. But perhaps there is a last opportunity for those who do not believe in Jesus in this life to make the choice to follow Him upon death. Just listen for the voice calling you to Him. It may not be a voice that is heard, but rather just the knowledge that He is calling out to you. Maybe, as I experienced, there is one last chance to follow the voice and the light that lead to Him. I believe that if we truly have faith in the love of Christ and the existence of life after death in eternity with Him, then we will die without fear and trembling. I can't imagine what it must be like to take the last breath of life thinking that life is finished, there is nothing more, all coherent awareness gone forever.

If Scripture is true, then it seems that our life here on earth is meant to prepare us for life in heaven. The key may be for us to learn how to love unconditionally, like Christ, so that we will be able to fit in with the harmony in heaven. But if Scripture is not true and it turns out to be the greatest hoax in the history of mankind, then the moment we die the lights go out, that's it, it's over, done, nothing. Maybe everything boils down to our very last thought as we take our very last breath. If that thought is about going to a perfect place that is overflowing with love and joy, then we will die well. Perhaps people who do not believe miss the connection with the lighted path to heaven as their spirit is not conditioned to respond.

I'm not sure where I heard the following words, but they hold great meaning to me:

We need our body to know the world around us. We need the soul to know ourselves. We need the spirit to know God.

We need our body to know the world around us. That's obvious. It takes our five senses in order to relate to our environment. *We need the soul to know ourselves.* Hmm… even though I had a near-death experience and many other close encounters with death, it took a divorce to break me to the point where contact by the Holy Spirit could get me to look at myself through an objective lens to get in touch with my heart, my soul. Then and only then was I able to really get to know myself. *We need the spirit to know God.* Yes, we do indeed. Perhaps that is why so many of us struggle with belief in God. Our bodies and minds are constantly bombarded with physical stimuli and worldly deception to the point where it takes a major effort to block out all the "static" in order to focus on the spirit.

I have come to the realization and understanding that we are not merely the image that we see when we look into a mirror. Our true and everlasting self is the spirit that inhabits the body that appears in the mirror. The Bible says in Genesis Chapter 2 that *God formed man from the dust of the ground and breathed into his nostrils the breath of life, and the man became a living being.* God's "breath of life" may refer to man's spirit, which lives on after the death of the body and which makes us different from the animals. Perhaps it is our spirit, the essence of our being, that is what God created in His image.

Yet not even the profound faith gained through the near-death experience while drowning was enough to change me. It was the power of Christ's love that produced the changes, some 23 years later. A thorough understanding of Jesus' gift of life is what allowed me to emerge from the cocoon.

The importance of love is expressed by the Apostle Paul in his first letter to the Corinthians (chapter 13:2); *If I have the gift of prophecy and can fathom all mysteries and all knowledge, and if I have a faith that can move mountains, but have not love, I am nothing.* My near-death experience provided me with unwavering faith in the existence of God and life after death, but it wasn't until I exposed my heart to Christ's true love that I was able to make a significant change in my life.

One of the most striking accomplishments of my transformation has been a complete overhaul of my understanding of what it means to love. I turned from a man whose attraction to women was primarily through the physical senses, particularly sight, to a man who fully appreciates their inner beauty. All of the women that I ever dated in all my life were women to whom I was very attracted physically. And then Tata came into my life. She is the only woman I've ever met that I was drawn to for the person she is deep down inside rather than what she appears to be on the surface. My relationship with Tata is one of the things that has taught me just how far I've come since emerging from my cocoon.

The greatest of all things is love; it is even greater than faith or hope (1Corinthians 13:13). From the definition of love in the Bible, it is clear that true love is something we choose to learn rather than just a feeling. *Love is patient, love is kind. It does not envy, it does not boast, it is not proud. It is not rude, it is not self-seeking, it is not easily angered, it keeps no record of wrongs* (1Corinthians 13:4-5).

We are not born with patience, as babies cry the instant they want something; we have to learn how to be patient. Kindness is something we learn how to express. One of the most difficult things for us to learn is how not to be self-serving. It often takes a conscious effort to resist the urge to envy or to boast, and it is difficult not to keep track of wrongs that have been done to us. And the ability to control anger takes a great deal of practice for many men to learn. Therefore, true love is more of something we have to *learn* rather than certain feelings we experience. The world tries to convince us that love is a *feeling* we have toward others. Yet that feeling often leads us into temptations and self-centeredness, which according to Scripture is not love.

The Bible says that God *is* love, so perhaps as we learn *how* to love we are actually learning about God; the more we know about love, the more we will know God. I suggest that God gave us the ability to enter into loving relationships with each other as a means for us to get to know Him in this life. There are many forms of love that we humans know and understand; the love between children and parents, the love between brother and sister, the love between friends, the love of life, the love of a beautiful sunset, the love of a favorite pet, the love of one's favorite flavor of ice cream. Oh, there are so many ways and things we can love! And the greatest of all forms of love is that which is the nature of Christ Jesus, that of *unconditional* love.

Since God is love and since we were created in His image, then it seems reasonable to conclude that if we take a look at all of the acts of kindness, of patience, of love, of pure selflessness throughout all of human history, perhaps then we will have a perception of the image and appearance of God.

References

Holy Bible. NIV Thinline Reference Bible. Zondervan, 2005.

Piper, Don and Cecil Murphey. *90 Minutes in Heaven*. Revell, 2004.